You, Your Friends, and Your Family

Vincent Bishop

Pour Tin qui sera toujours tous les deux F pour moi.

Published in 2001 by The Rosen Publishing Group, Inc.
29 East 21st Street, New York, NY 10010

Copyright © 2001 by The Rosen Publishing Group, Inc.

First Edition

All rights reserved. No part of this book may be reproduced in any form without permission in writing from the publisher, except by a reviewer.

Library of Congress Cataloging-in-Publication Data

Bishop, Vincent.
You, your friends, and your family/Vincent Bishop—1st ed.
    p. cm.—(Family matters)
  ISBN: 978-1-4358-3617-4
  1. Parent and teenager—Juvenile literature. 2. Communication in the family—Juvenile literature. 3. Teenagers—Family relationships—Juvenile literature. 4. Interpersonal relations in adolescence—Juvenile literature. 5. Friendship—Juvenile literature. [1. Adolescence. 2. Parent and teenager. 3. Interpersonal relations. 4. Family life. 5. Friendship.] I. Title. II. Family matters (New York, N.Y.)
   HQ799.15 .B57 2000
   306.874—dc21

                                                            00-010643

Manufactured in the United States of America

Contents

	Introduction	5
1	You and Your Parents	7
2	You and Your Friends	17
3	Sisters and Brothers	27
4	Out and About	35
	Glossary	42
	For More Information	43
	For Further Reading	46
	Index	47

During your teenage years, your relationships with your family and your friends are both probably very important to you.

Introduction

Changes can be great. However, they can also cause problems. At your age, you are changing a lot, and your relationships with your family and your friends are changing too. Both friends and family are probably very important to you. But what do you do when there are problems between them?

What if your dad kicks your new friend out of the house? What if your best friend gets a big crush on your older brother and starts ignoring you? Can peer pressure at school really have an impact on the way you act at home?

As you become older and you start gaining more independence, there are bound to be conflicts between you, your family, and your friends. This book will take a look at some examples of such conflicts, and will explore different ways kids and grown-ups can communicate effectively with each other. There are usually several ways of solving a problem. Hopefully, this book will give you some ideas of what to do, and what not to do, so that everybody in your family can get along well (at least most of the time).

After all, your family matters, and though growing up can be tough, good communication will make your day-to-day interactions run more smoothly.

You and Your Parents

Do you feel different around your parents lately? Do you snap at your mom for no reason when she asks if those are the pants you're going to wear to Lee's birthday party? Do you wish you were living on another continent when your Dad shows up at your hockey game in that ridiculous purple Barney hat your little sister gave him for Father's Day?

What's with them anyway? How come they've changed? They never used to be so nosy, annoying, interfering, and embarrassing. A year or two ago, you liked spending time with them. Now, you almost have to push them away sometimes. It's as if they don't want to let you live your own life.

The funny thing is that it's probably not your parents who have done the changing. It's you.

When you were younger, you probably spent a lot more time with your parent or parents.

My, How You've Changed

Until your middle school years your life was probably simpler. You were a little kid. Your parents more or less ran your life. Although you might have hung out with friends from school, clubs, or in your neighborhood, you probably spent a fair amount of your free time with one or both parents. After all, there are some things you can just be too young to do without a parent or an older sibling around.

Once you hit your double digits, however, things begin to change. You're older for one thing. You're bigger, smarter, more experienced, and more responsible. And you'll probably be craving more independence—both inside and outside your home. An important part of this is standing on your own two feet, without your parents always hovering over you. It's not that you love your parents any less. It's just that you don't need or want them around so much. You also want to build new relationships on your own. The most important new relationships you will have are friendships.

An Exciting and Complicated Time

Good, solid friendships with kids your own age, who are going through the same things you are, can be one of the best things in life. Whether shooting lay-ups or darts, trading baseball cards or secrets, or even just hanging out and goofing around, there are many things that you can only do—and will only want to do—with your friends.

This time in your life can be exciting. It can also be complicated. Although you might want to share some information about your new independent life and your friends with your family, you probably don't want to share everything. It is your life and it's quite natural to want a bit of privacy. At the same time, adjusting to your new independence and new friends can be difficult for your parents.

Think of it from their point of view. Up until now, they knew most things about your life—including the people in it. Your parents were, and they still are, responsible for taking care of you. Then suddenly, you're home a lot less. You're also probably spending more time listening to and confiding in friends than you are with your folks. Parents might feel a little hurt, left out, or worried. After all, your growing up is a unique experience not just for you but for everybody in your family. And even though they're grown-ups, parents are also humans with feelings and doubts.

When Valerie was talking to Shanice on the bedroom extension, she heard a click. Nobody was home except her dad. Could he really be listening in on her phone conversation? Shanice was going on about how much she hated her mother's new boyfriend. At least Shanice had a mother. Since Valerie's mom died a year ago, it had just been her and her dad. And things had been sort of distant between them. As soon as Shanice finished complaining, Valerie made an excuse and said she had to get off the phone. Then she tore downstairs.

"You were listening in on my phone conversation!" Valerie screamed.

Her dad didn't say anything.

"Well? What's your problem?" demanded Valerie.

"Nothing," mumbled her dad.

"What do you mean 'nothing'?" Valerie was furious.

"Okay, then. The problem is you," said her father. "Since your mom died, we never see each other. I'm at work. You're never around. But even when both of us are home, you never talk to me anymore. It's always Shanice this and Shanice that. You spend more time at Shanice's than here."

It's normal for teenagers to argue with parents over issues like privacy.

"So what? She's my best friend."

"I just want to know what's going on in your life."

"And that gives you the right to eavesdrop?"

Valerie stomped out of the house and went over to Shanice's. She hated her dad and hated being at home. Not that it was much of a home anymore with her mom gone and her dad always moping around. Shanice's house felt more like home.

It's not unusual for communication with your parents to become more difficult. You want to spend more time on your own and with your friends. As you begin to have more experiences outside of your household, and you see what goes on in your friends' homes, you'll start to look at your home and parents with new eyes. Up until now, your home and your family were the norm. Now you begin comparing different styles of living and different styles of parenting. Why does your mom ground you for being fifteen minutes late for dinner when Freda's mom lets Freda eat whatever she wants, whenever she wants? Why doesn't your dad play basketball with you and your friends like Tony's dad does? Comparisons such as these might cause you to view your parents critically for the first time. The way you express such criticisms could lead to arguments.

Valerie slept over at Shanice's house that night. Although actually, she didn't sleep much at all. Valerie felt guilty about blowing up at her dad. He had no right to listen in on her phone conversations or to criticize her for hanging out with Shanice. But it was true that Valerie rarely told her dad stuff anymore. She talked much more to Shanice's mom than to her own dad. And she was never at home. Even Shanice thought that was weird. "How come we don't go to your place?" she'd ask Valerie. Valerie would make some excuse about her father not liking noise in the house. But the real reason was she didn't want Shanice to see her father acting so depressed.

The next day after school, Valerie was nervous about going home. When she got there her dad was sitting in the kitchen, that same sad look on his face.

"I'm really sorry I listened in on your phone conversation," he said. "And I'm glad you have a good friend like Shanice. I know she's been a big support to you. I guess I just miss your mom, but I don't want to lose you too."

"I miss you too, Daddy," said Valerie. "I really like hanging out with Shanice, but I promise to stay around a bit more."

Five Ways to Keep the Lines of Communication Open

Sure, you and your parents are going to get into arguments. From time to time, that can even be a good thing. If something is eating away at you, it's better to get it off your chest than to stew, brood, and pretend that nothing is wrong. The same goes for your parents. However, some ways of communicating are better than others.

1. **Don't scream, yell, or rant.** Your parents will react to your tone of voice instead of to what you are actually saying.

2. **Don't slam the door to your room or stomp out of the house.** Sort of immature, don't you think?

3. **Use "I" messages instead of blaming another person.** Instead of saying "You're always treating me as if I'm a little kid," try "I think you sometimes treat me as if I'm a little kid." The first phrase puts your parent on the defensive. The second allows for discussion and resolution of a problem.

4. **Consider your parents' feelings and point of view.** Valerie was furious that her dad eavesdropped, but once she saw his side of things, she realized they both had made mistakes.

5. **Try to compromise.** It helps a lot when each side feels that the other is willing to make an effort. Valerie's willingness to spend more time at home with her dad, along with her dad's support for her strong friendship with Shanice, allowed them to compromise.

As more and more of your life takes place beyond the walls of your own home, you will be exposed to new ideas and people. Other things and people—especially friends and teachers—will influence your opinions and beliefs. Some influences might be good, others bad. Sometimes, your parents might not share your new ideas. They might even argue with you about them. Maybe they don't think some of your recent opinions or ways of behaving are very positive.

Let's say one of your friends has a problem with people he believes are homosexuals. Maybe he goes around calling people "faggots." Maybe, without really thinking about it, you begin doing this too. Your parents might be critical of what they view as a prejudiced attitude. They might be critical of your friend, too. Do you think they would have good reason to be critical?

In middle school, you will probably meet all kinds of people, including those with backgrounds, interests, and personalities different from yours.

You and Your Friends

Once you're in middle school, there will likely be different kids in every class you take. You might get involved in more clubs and extra-curricular activities. All of this means you'll be exposed to many more kids—kids with different backgrounds, interests, and personalities. The number and variety of potential new friends can be overwhelming. At the same time, relationships with old friends might go through some changes. Sometimes you might drift apart for a while. Other times you might drift apart for good.

Clark and Shelli had been best friends since kindergarten. Their mothers were best friends from high school. Because their mothers spent so much time together, Clark and Shelli did too. They even went to the same school. Once, Shelli overheard her mom talking to Clark's mom. She was saying how happy it made her that their kids had become such close friends.

Once Clark and Shelli entered junior high, they were suddenly busier. Clark joined the Boy Scouts and started hanging out with some guys who didn't like girls all that much. Shelli didn't care. She got into ceramics and made some new friends who had nothing in common with Clark and his pals.

One day, Shelli's mom invited Shelli to go to a play with her. "You can call Clark, too," she suggested.

"I'd rather invite Ramona," said Shelli.

"But hon, you and Clark are such good friends. It makes me sad that you never see each other."

"Mom, Clark and I really don't have anything in common anymore."

Shelli's mom looked sad.

"I'd really like you to meet Ramona," said Shelli.

"Okay, hon," said Shelli's mother. "I'd like to meet Ramona, too."

It's nice if your parents approve of your friends, but not so nice if they try to choose your friends. Nonetheless, it's important that your parents meet your friends and know who you are hanging around with. If your family is an important part of your life and your friends are as well, it's only normal that they know each other. After all, they have an important thing in common—you.

Making friends can be tough. At your age, kids' interests, likes, and dislikes can change not only from year to year, but month to month, or even from one week to the next. Some kids change friends like they change clothes. A good friend is someone who stands by you no matter what, someone you can trust, and someone who accepts you for who you are. This is the most basic, but often most ignored, trick to winning and keeping friends: Don't try to act "cool," don't try to impress people; just be yourself.

When Rob's family moved, it seemed as if he'd never make any friends at his new school. The only one who made an effort to get to know Rob was Baxter. Baxter wore thick glasses, weighed 150 pounds, and knew the names of all the Roman Emperors by heart. Rob definitely didn't want to get lumped in with him.

Instead, he wanted to be friends with Cyrus, Matt, and Rita. They were known as the South Doors Gang. He took to hanging out with them at the south doors, where he'd offer everyone

Sometimes the desire to fit in can cause you to make self-destructive choices.

some of the cigars he had stolen from the corner store. It made Rob feel great that he was in with this clique.

One day after school, Cyrus said they should walk home together. At Rob's house, Cyrus asked if he could come in. Rob hesitated. Even though Cyrus was cool, Rob wondered if his parents would approve of him. Rob also worried that Cyrus might think his family was nerdy. Cyrus' dad was a bartender and had once dated Madonna.

"Come on, man!" coaxed Cyrus, as they stood on the front porch. So Rob pulled out his key and opened the door.

Immediately, he wished he hadn't. A Celine Dion CD was playing in the living room.

"Who listens to that stuff?" asked Cyrus, a disgusted look on his face.

"Uh . . . the cleaning lady must have left it on," muttered Rob, running to turn the stereo off. "She's really tacky."

Rob started leading Cyrus upstairs when his little brother Max appeared.

"Hey Rob!" yelled Max. "Up for a game of ping pong?"

"Who's that little creep?" asked Cyrus.

"Get lost, loser," snarled Rob, pushing past his brother. He was secretly horrified that Max had let it

slip that he played such a geeky game. Without another word, he took Cyrus up to his room.

Once they were locked inside, Cyrus pulled out some smokes. He fired one up before handing one to Rob. Rob had never smoked before, and he certainly didn't want to smoke in the house. He knew his dad would kill him. But he didn't want to act like a wuss in front of Cyrus.

No sooner had he lit up, when there was a pounding on the door. "Robster?"

Don't be surprised if your parent tries to stop you from doing something you shouldn't!

Rob jumped up in a panic. "Quick! Put out your smoke!" he pleaded with Cyrus.

"Robster?" mimicked Cyrus with a sneer.

"Open the door!" yelled Rob's dad.

Rob opened the door and his dad barged in.

"Yo, Daddy-o!" said Cyrus, with a fake salute.

>*Rob's dad ignored him. Instead he turned to Rob. "What is with being mean to your brother and turning off my music? And, more importantly, why do I smell cigarette smoke?"*
>
>*"Just ask Robster here," answered Cyrus, barely able to suppress a laugh. "He thought the CD belonged to the cleaning lady."*
>
>*"What cleaning lady?" asked Rob's dad. "Rob, I want to know why you're acting like this. As for you," he said, looking at Cyrus, "I'd like you to leave, please."*
>
>*"Dad, you can't order my friends around."*
>
>*"Whoever said we were friends, Robster?" asked Cyrus, as he walked past Rob's dad, stomped downstairs and out the door.*

Everybody wants to belong. It hurts to be on the outside. But as Rob discovered, it can hurt to be on the inside, too, if you have to pretend to be someone that you're not. Okay, let's face it. Maybe your younger brother is into stuff you think is immature. But that doesn't mean he's a loser. After all, he is younger. And maybe your parents do stuff that embarrasses you from time to time. But is it really such a crime to listen to Celine Dion? Everybody has his or her own likes and dislikes. Your dad might think 'N Sync is horrible and your mom might think your baggy cargo pants look ridiculous. They might even tell you so. Which is fine. Everybody has a right to their own opinion, especially your parents. But do you really think they would treat you differently or disown you in public because of your tastes? It's okay to realize that you and your parents are different in some ways. But it's essential to respect each other's differences.

Some friendships might last years. Others might last a week. Your family lasts forever. They are an essential part of your life and you have to seriously question any friendship that is going to have a negative impact on your relationship with your parents and siblings. If you have to hide your family, or act differently with them just to impress a friend, that friend isn't worth it. In your life, you'll have many, many friends. You'll only have one family.

Do you think Rob's dad was right in telling Cyrus to leave his house? He could claim that Cyrus was rude, that he smoked cigarettes, and that he seemed to be a bad influence on Rob. Smoking, drinking alcohol, and taking drugs are dangerous habits that could lead to serious addiction, disease, and death. More and more kids your age are being tempted by these habits. Even if they sometimes act strict or overprotective, your parents have every right to worry about your health and safety. It's something you should be worried about, too. Although he didn't tell Rob not to be friends with Cyrus, Rob's dad did make it clear he didn't want Cyrus in his house. Although Rob might have been annoyed that his dad made Cyrus leave, he can't deny that Cyrus behaved badly to his family.

Cliques and Geeks

Like Rob, lots of kids your age feel they have to look or behave a certain way to fit in. Some kids even insist that

Peer pressure can sometimes cause you to feel as if you should look or behave in a certain way.

A Clique . . .	A Group of Friends . . .
Excludes others	Includes others
Wants everyone to be the same	Doesn't mind if people are different
Looks down on others outside the clique	Likes other people outside the group
Has to do everything together	Does some things together and other things apart

you look or behave in a certain way or else they'll have nothing to do with you. This is called peer pressure and it's a big problem most kids face. Sometimes your parents, who are more experienced, might see the effects of peer pressure on you more than you do. If they criticize what they see as negative behavior or a poor choice in friends, they might have a good reason. You should at least hear them out. They only want what's best for you.

A lot of peer pressure comes from cliques. A clique is a small group of kids that excludes other kids. Basically, cliques think anybody that doesn't look, dress, or act like them is a geek. Although a clique is a group, there's a big difference between being part of a clique and being part of a group of friends.

Brothers and sisters are a big part of your life, and as you grow older, your relationships with your siblings will probably change.

Sisters and Brothers

Most kids have strong relationships with their siblings. Whether you argue with them, ignore them, or are the best of buds with them, brothers and sisters are a big part of your life. When you hit your double digits and your world begins changing, your relationship with your siblings will probably change, too.

Younger Sibling Troubles

Rachel, twelve, and her brother Julian, ten, had always spent a lot of time together. Rachel was a tomboy and she and Julian had a group of guys in the neighborhood with whom they played softball and kick-the-can all the time.

Then Rachel went off to junior high and started hanging out with girls. Julian was shocked when Rachel started wearing skirts and grew her hair out.

Julian felt that Rachel wasn't interested in him anymore. She spent a lot of time at her new friend Sheena's house and she never wanted to do anything together like they used to. Julian hated Sheena. Once, she had mussed his hair and called him a "small fry." He decided that if Rachel was going to ignore him, he would ignore her too.

Rachel didn't really miss the neighborhood kids. They were nice and everything, but pretty immature. Julian was being a big pain, though. He was always sulky around her. And he was pretty rude to her friend Sheena. Thinking he was going through a phase, Rachel decided just to ignore Julian until he grew out of it.

Because you and your siblings are growing up at different rates, it's inevitable that at some periods you'll be much closer and have more things in common than at other periods. Because you're different people, you'll have different types of friends. When you're in your early teens, you'll naturally gravitate more to kids your own age, who share your classes, gossip, problems, and interests. Even a small age gap of two years can seem large when you're twelve and fourteen or thirteen and fifteen.

Of course, you have to expect that while you're out discovering your independence and making new pals, your younger brother or sister might feel a bit left out, especially if the two of you used to spend a lot of time together. He or she might feel jealous of new friends who take up all your time and envious of the new freedoms you have, such as going out more and staying up later. Sure, you don't want your little brother tagging along when you go to the movies with your friends. However, while there are many things that you want to do alone with your new friends, it doesn't mean that you have to act as if your siblings are as insignificant and annoying as mosquitoes. Even if they are obnoxious at times, they probably look up to you—even if they'd never admit it. And being cool with your little sister or brother now can pave the way for a strong friendship when you hit twenty and twenty-two or thirty and thirty-two (at which point, the age gap basically disappears).

OLDER SIBLING TROUBLES

While younger siblings can be a source of problems at times, so can older siblings, albeit for different reasons.

Your younger siblings probably look up to you, so try not to always exclude them.

The first time Ana brought her friend Jennifer over to her apartment, they had a great time. At least until Jennifer caught sight of Ana's sixteen-year-old brother Manuel. "He's cute!" exclaimed Jennifer, her eyes practically popping out of her head. "He looks just like Ricky Martin!" Even though Manuel barely gave either of them the time of day—he was too busy fixing his bike out in the parking lot—Jennifer was so gooey over him that Ana was embarrassed. When Jennifer asked if she could have a soda out of the fridge, Ana said of course. She didn't suspect that Jen would take the soda out to Manuel and spend twenty minutes talking to him in the parking lot. And what did Manuel think he was up to, taking off his shirt in the middle of the conversation? Kind of stupid to show off his muscles when it was fifty degrees outside.

When Jennifer finally came back inside, Ana was seething but she played it cool. "Where were you?" she asked her friend. "Oh, Ana, your brother's so great," gushed Jennifer. "He's going to take me for a ride on his bike when he gets it fixed up."

"Great," muttered Ana, and vowed not to invite Jen over again unless she knew Manuel would be out. A couple of days later, however, the phone rang.

It can be tough if one of your friends becomes romantically involved with your sibling.

Ana's mother answered it and said, "It's Jennifer." Ana moved to take the receiver, but her Mom said, "It's not for you, Annie. It's for Manuel."

When her brother got off the phone, Ana was ready to kill him. "What did Jen want?" Ana demanded.

"She wants me to come over and watch a video."

"All alone? She didn't invite me, too?" Ana couldn't believe it.

"Nope."

"That traitor!" Ana was angry. "You're not going, are you?"

"Well . . ." said Manuel teasingly.

"You'd better not. She's my friend! You better stop leading her on!"

"Hey, cool it, Ana," Manuel interrupted her and laid a hand on his sister's shoulder. "I'm not going over there. I'm not interested in your little friends."

In most situations like Ana's, an older sibling probably won't be interested in a "little kid" with a crush. However, he or she might be kind of flattered by the attention. And obviously it's not a very nice situation for you to feel like an outsider around your sibling and your (supposed) pal. If it looks as if your friend's infatuation isn't going to blow over anytime soon, it's probably a good idea to try talking to both your older sibling and your friend. Manuel didn't take Jen's crush very seriously, but Ana did. When he saw how hurt and angry she was, he made it clear he wasn't interested in Jen. Hopefully, he'll find a way of (nicely) making it clear to Jen as well.

Ana, however, shouldn't have tried to act as if there was nothing wrong when her friend showed interest in Manuel. Without getting mad, calling her a traitor, and showing how green with envy the situation made her, she could have mentioned to Jen that she felt hurt by the fact that Jen had invited Manuel to watch a video without inviting her. If Jen is really a good friend, she will take Ana's hurt feelings into consideration and won't put her in a similar situation in the future. Of course, Jen might take Ana's feelings into consideration but still decide she wants to pursue Manuel. If Ana can't accept that, they are going to have a big problem. Jen will have to decide which means more to her—her friend, or the remote possibility of getting together with Manuel.

Most parents will allow their kids more independence, or freedom, as their children grow older.

Out and About

Growing older means gaining more independence. Most parents are okay about allowing their kids more freedom. Usually what they expect in return is responsible behavior. If they allow you to go out with your friends until 9 PM, they expect you to be home by 9 PM. If you turn up at 10 PM, you show your parents that you're not responsible and that you can't be trusted. The less parents can trust you, the more they will worry about you when you are out of the house. In general, the key to getting more freedom is to prove that you are a responsible person.

> *Even before she asked permission, Jan knew her mother was going to make a stink about her going to Clement's party. She was right. Ever since her older brother Charlie was killed in an accidental shooting, her mom had turned into this major worrier.*

"I don't want you going," she said. "I bet there will be drugs and alcohol there and you never know what kind of trouble that could lead to."

Jan was ready for her though. She knew that if she made a big fuss and accused her mom of being unfair, she would just put her foot down even more. Instead, in a calm voice, she tried another tactic.

"Look, Mom, this party's really important to me. If it will make you feel better, you can drive me there and we'll arrange a time beforehand for you to come pick me up. Clement's parents are going to be home that night. If you want, I can give you their number and you can talk to them."

Although she didn't look totally happy about it, Jan's mother found her daughter's offer pretty much impossible to refuse.

Even overprotective parents who worry too much will usually be willing to compromise if you can make them see that they have nothing to worry about. Although many parents have trouble getting used to the fact that their "babies" prefer to cruise the mall with their buds than hang out at home playing a family game of Scrabble, at the same time many parents are proud of their children's newfound independence.

Of course, parents are going to worry about you as you spend more time out of their sight. After all, they care

Party Time!

Teenage parties are legendary. Many kids live for them, and many parents fear them. Getting together with your parents and working out some party rules ahead of time can be a good idea.

Tips for Going to a Party

Agree on your curfew ahead of time and stick to it.

Tell your parents where the party is and who is going to be there, and give them the number of your friend's parents' house.

Assure them that you won't be doing any drinking or using any drugs.

Tips for Having a Party

Parents should be seen—they can make their presence known and then disappear to another part of the house—but not heard—no lingering around to hang out with your buds.

No drugs, alcohol, or cigarettes.

No party crashers—your parents should know how many kids are expected and more or less who these people are.

Agree on a time that everybody clears out.

about your safety and things are a lot more dangerous in some ways than when they were your age. More kids have access to guns and other weapons. Drugs and alcohol are a bigger problem at a younger age. And playing in the streets or in a park can bring you into contact with muggers, rapists, gangs, and other threatening figures.

You can cut down on your parents' worries, and in doing so cut yourself some slack, by being a good communicator. Always let your folks know where you are going to be, for how long, and what time you'll be home. If these plans change, call them and ask if it's okay to stay an hour longer at the park or to eat dinner at your friend's house. If possible, give them a number where you can be reached. This will ease their minds and let them know you are responsible and that you respect their concerns.

Duane had come over to Avi's place several times and he seemed to hit it off pretty well with Avi's parents. At least that's what Avi had thought. But when he asked his parents if he could go over to Duane's place and spend the night there, his parents exchanged funny looks and said no.

"What do you mean, 'No'?" asked Avi. "Duane's parents let him come over here."

"That's different, son," said Avi's dad. "This is a pretty safe neighborhood. Duane's neighborhood is one of the worst areas for violent crime in the city."

"Well, Duane hangs out in his 'hood."

"Avi," said his mom. "Duane's neighborhood is mostly black and Duane is black, too. You're not."

"So he can come over here to our mostly white neighborhood, but I can't go over there to his mostly black neighborhood. I think that's really racist," said Avi.

"It's not because it's a mostly black neighborhood that we're concerned, Avi. It's because it's an unsafe neighborhood," said Avi's dad. "We'd be just as concerned about you going to a mostly white neighborhood if it was known to be unsafe."

"We like Duane a lot," explained Avi's mom. "But we would prefer if you had him sleep over here instead. Would that be a big problem?"

"I don't know. I'll have to think about it and then talk to Duane," said Avi.

You won't always agree with your parents' decisions or attitudes. But you are their child and they do have the right to make rules. Hopefully, these rules

Sometimes you will not share your parents' view of the way the world is.

are based on concern for your safety and well-being. Although Avi wasn't thrilled by his parents' argument, at least they explained their reasons and offered him another option. Then it's his choice whether or not to accept that option. Of course, parents are human and not always perfect. They might have ideas or opinions you really don't agree with and know are wrong. And they might not be willing to compromise.

When Josh brought Nick over to his house for the first time, his dad acted as if Nick didn't exist. Nick was black, and Josh's dad didn't like black people. Josh was really embarrassed by his dad's rude behavior.

After Nick went home, Josh's dad wanted to talk to Josh. "I don't want that person in my house," he said.

"Why not?" asked Josh.

"He's black and we're not, and that's enough," said his dad abruptly.

Josh was upset. He loved his dad, but his dad was really prejudiced. Josh decided to talk to his mom.

"Your father is a good person," said Josh's mom. "But, like everybody, he has his flaws. He has some opinions about people that you and I don't share. And unfortunately, he's probably not going to change."

"So you're saying I can't have Nick over to our house?" demanded Josh.

You don't need to share a parent's prejudices.

"Josh, if your father doesn't want Nick in his house, there is nothing you and I can do about it," sighed Josh's mom. *"Nick wouldn't feel comfortable here, anyway. That doesn't mean you have to stop being friends with Nick. I'm glad that you can see beyond skin color. You must get that from your mom."*

Navigating the sometimes rough waters between your friends and your family can be a delicate task. It takes patience, understanding, flexibility, and good communication. Sure, your parents can be a pain from time to time. And friends can be flaky, flighty, or even kind of mean at times. But it sure is better to have them than to be without them.

Glossary

clique   Small, select group that excludes others based on how they look

compromise   When two parties each give something up to resolve their differences.

curfew   Set hour to be at home.

excluded   To be left out.

homosexual   Someone who is physically and emotionally attracted to people of the same sex.

immature   Not very grown-up.

norm   Standard, average.

options   Choices.

peer pressure   When you feel forced into something by kids your own age.

For More Information

IN THE UNITED STATES

Al-Anon/Alateen
1600 Corporate Landing Parkway
Virginia Beach, VA 23454-5617
(888) 4AL-ANON (425-2666)
Web site: http://www.al-anon-alateen.org

Big Brothers Big Sisters of America
230 North 13th Street
Philadelphia, PA 19107
(215) 567-7000
e-mail: national@bbbsa.org
Web site: http://www.bbbsa.org

Covenant House Nine Line
(800) 999-9999
Web site: http://www.covenanthouse.org

Families Anonymous
P.O. Box 3475
Culver City, CA 90231-3475
(800) 736-9805
e-mail: famanon@familiesanonymous.org
Web site: http://www.familiesanonymous.org

Families with Children
Hospice of the North Shore
2821 Central Street
Evanston, IL 60201
(847) HOSPICE (467-7423)
e-mail: careinfo@carecenter.org
Web site: http://www.carecenter.org

Join Together
441 Stuart Street
Boston, MA 02116
(617) 437-1500
e-mail: info@jointogether.org
Web site: http://www.jointogether.org

Siblings Understanding Needs (SUN)
Department of Pediatrics C-19
University of Texas Medical Branch
Galveston, TX 77550

IN CANADA

Big Brothers and Sisters of Canada
3228 South Service Road, Suite 113E
Burlington, ON L7N 3H8
(800) 263-9133
e-mail: bbsc@bbbsc.ca
Web site: http://www.bbsc.ca

Canadian Public Health Association
1565 Carling Avenue, Suite 400
Ottawa, ON K1Z 8R1
(613) 725-3769
e-mail: info@cpha.ca
Web site: http://www.cpha.ca

For Further Reading

Hersch, Patricia. *A Tribe Apart: A Journey into the Heart of American Adolescence.* New York: Ballantine Books, 1999.

Mosatche, Harriet S., and Karen Unger. *Too Old for This, Too Young for That.* Minneapolis, MN: Free Spirit Publishing, 2000.

Ré, Judith. *Social Savvy: A Handbook for Teens Who Want to Know What to Say, What to Do, and How to Feel Confident in Any Situation.* New York: Summit Books, 1992.

Parsons, Alexandra, and Peter Sanders. *It's My Life.* Danbury, CT: Franklin Watts, 1997.

Romain, Trevor. *Cliques, Phonies, & Other Baloney.* Minneapolis, MN: Free Spirit Publishing, 1998.

Schwartz, Linda. *What Do You Think? A Kid's Guide to Dealing With Daily Dilemmas.* Minneapolis, MN: Learning Works, 1993.

Sommers, Michael. *Chillin': The Guy's Guide to Friendship.* New York: The Rosen Publishing Group, 2000.

Index

A
alcohol, drinking, 24, 37
arguments, getting into, 12, 14, 27

B
being yourself, 19, 22
blaming others, 14

C
changes, going through, 5, 7, 8–9, 17, 27
cliques, 24–25
communication, 6, 12, 14, 32–33, 38, 41
compromising, 14, 36, 40
conflicts, 5–6
crushes, 5, 32, 33

D
drugs, 24, 37, 38

F
feelings, 9, 14, 33
fitting in, 22, 24–25
friends, 5, 8, 9, 12, 14, 15, 17–25, 28–29, 32–33, 36, 41
   being a bad influence, 15, 24
   relationships with new, 9, 13, 17, 28, 29

I
independence, gaining, 5, 8, 9, 28, 35, 36

P
parents, 5, 7–15, 18, 22–23, 25, 35–41
  being responsible for you, 8, 9
  disapproving of your friends, 5, 9, 15, 25
  overprotective, 24, 36
  worrying about you, 9, 35, 36–38, 40
parties, tips for, 37
peer pressure, 5, 25
privacy, wanting, 9, 29
problem solving, 6, 14

R
respect for others, 24, 38

responsible behavior, 35
rules, 39–40

S
school, 5, 8, 17
siblings, 5, 8, 22, 24, 27–33
  age gap, 28, 29
  feeling left out, 29, 32
  older, 29–33
  younger, 22, 27–29
smoking, 24, 37

T
teachers, being an influence, 13–15
trust, gaining it, 19, 35

About the Author

Vincent Bishop has worked as a taxi driver and a painter. He is currently a writer for Web sites and the father of three teenagers.

Photo Credits

Cover and interior shots by Ira Fox.

Design and Layout

Geri Giordano

www.ingramcontent.com/pod-product-compliance
Lightning Source LLC
Chambersburg PA
CBHW041117070526

44584CB00002B/192